DOCTOR FAUSTUS

Christopher Marlowe

EDITORIAL DIRECTOR Laurie Barnett
DIRECTOR OF TECHNOLOGY Tammy Hepps

SERIES EDITOR John Crowther
MANAGING EDITOR Vincent Janoski

WRITERS Rebecca Gaines, Ross Douthat
EDITORS Dennis Quinio, Benjamin Morgan

This edition published by Spark Publishing

Spark Publishing
A Division of SparkNotes LLC
120 Fifth Avenue, 8th Floor
New York, NY 10011

Please submit all comments and questions or report errors to www.sparknotes.com/errors

Printed and bound in the United States

ISBN 1-58663-508-5

INTRODUCTION: STOPPING TO BUY SPARKNOTES ON A SNOWY EVENING

Whose words these are you *think* you know.
Your paper's due tomorrow, though;
We're glad to see you stopping here
To get some help before you go.

Lost your course? You'll find it here.
Face tests and essays without fear.
Between the words, good grades at stake:
Get great results throughout the year.

Once school bells caused your heart to quake
As teachers circled each mistake.
Use SparkNotes and no longer weep,
Ace every single test you take.

Yes, books are lovely, dark, and deep,
But only what you grasp you keep,
With hours to go before you sleep,
With hours to go before you sleep.

CONTENTS

CONTEXT

ORN IN CANTERBURY IN 1564, the same year as William Shakespeare, Christopher Marlowe was an actor, poet, and playwright during the reign of Britain's Queen Elizabeth I (ruled 1558–1603). Marlowe attended Corpus Christi College at Cambridge University and received degrees in 1584 and 1587. Traditionally, the education that he received would have prepared him to become a clergyman, but Marlowe chose not to join the ministry. For a time, Cambridge even wanted to withhold his degree, apparently suspecting him of having converted to Catholicism, a forbidden faith in late-sixteenth-century England, where Protestantism was the state-supported religion. Queen Elizabeth's Privy Council intervened on his behalf, saying that Marlowe had "done her majesty good service" in "matters touching the benefit of the country." This odd sequence of events has led some to theorize that Marlowe worked as a spy for the crown, possibly by infiltrating Catholic communities in France.

After leaving Cambridge, Marlowe moved to London, where he became a playwright and led a turbulent, scandal-plagued life. He produced seven plays, all of which were immensely popular. Among the most well known of his plays are *Tamburlaine*, *The Jew of Malta*, and *Doctor Faustus*. In his writing, he pioneered the use of blank verse—nonrhyming lines of iambic pentameter—which many of his contemporaries, including William Shakespeare, later adopted. In 1593, however, Marlowe's career was cut short. After being accused of heresy (maintaining beliefs contrary to those of an approved religion), he was arrested and put on a sort of probation. On May 30, 1593, shortly after being released, Marlowe became involved in a tavern brawl and was killed when one of the combatants stabbed him in the head. After his death, rumors were spread accusing him of treason, atheism, and homosexuality, and some people speculated that the tavern brawl might have been the work of government agents. Little evidence to support these allegations has come to light, however.

Doctor Faustus was probably written in 1592, although the exact date of its composition is uncertain, since it was not published until a decade later. The idea of an individual selling his or her soul to the devil for knowledge is an old motif in Christian folklore, one that had become attached to the historical persona of Johannes Faustus, a disreputable astrologer who lived in Germany sometime in the early 1500s. The immediate source of Marlowe's play seems to be the anonymous German work Historia von D. Iohan Fausten of 1587, which was translated into English in 1592, and from which Marlowe lifted the bulk of the plot for his drama. Although there had been literary representations of Faust prior to Marlowe's play, *Doctor Faustus* is the first famous version of the story. Later versions include the long and famous poem Faust by the nineteenth-century Romantic writer Johann Wolfgang von Goethe, as well as operas by Charles Gounod and Arrigo Boito and a symphony by Hector Berlioz. Meanwhile, the phrase "Faustian bargain" has entered the English lexicon, referring to any deal made for a short-term gain with great costs in the long run.

PLOT OVERVIEW

DOCTOR FAUSTUS, A WELL-RESPECTED GERMAN scholar, grows dissatisfied with the limits of traditional forms of knowledge—logic, medicine, law, and religion—and decides that he wants to learn to practice magic. His friends Valdes and Cornelius instruct him in the black arts, and he begins his new career as a magician by summoning up Mephastophilis, a devil. Despite Mephastophilis's warnings about the horrors of hell, Faustus tells the devil to return to his master, Lucifer, with an offer of Faustus's soul in exchange for twenty-four years of service from Mephastophilis. Meanwhile, Wagner, Faustus's servant, has picked up some magical ability and uses it to press a clown named Robin into his service.

Mephastophilis returns to Faustus with word that Lucifer has accepted Faustus's offer. Faustus experiences some misgivings and wonders if he should repent and save his soul; in the end, though, he agrees to the deal, signing it with his blood. As soon as he does so, the words "Homo fuge," Latin for "O man, fly," appear branded on his arm. Faustus again has second thoughts, but Mephastophilis bestows rich gifts on him and gives him a book of spells to learn. Later, Mephastophilis answers all of his questions about the nature of the world, refusing to answer only when Faustus asks him who made the universe. This refusal prompts yet another bout of misgivings in Faustus, but Mephastophilis and Lucifer bring in personifications of the Seven Deadly Sins to prance about in front of Faustus, and he is impressed enough to quiet his doubts.

Armed with his new powers and attended by Mephastophilis, Faustus begins to travel. He goes to the pope's court in Rome, makes himself invisible, and plays a series of tricks. He disrupts the pope's banquet by stealing food and boxing the pope's ears. Following this incident, he travels through the courts of Europe, with his fame spreading as he goes. Eventually, he is invited to the court of the German emperor, Charles V (the enemy of the pope), who asks Faustus to allow him to see Alexander the Great, the famed fourth-century B.C. Macedonian king and conqueror. Faustus conjures up an image of Alexander, and Charles is suitably impressed. A knight scoffs at Faustus's powers, and Faustus chastises him by making antlers sprout from his head. Furious, the knight vows revenge.

Meanwhile, Robin, Wagner's clown, has picked up some magic on his own, and with his fellow stablehand, Rafe, he undergoes a number of comic misadventures. At one point, he manages to summon Mephastophilis, who threatens to turn Robin and Rafe into animals (or perhaps even does transform them; the text isn't clear) to punish them for their foolishness.

Faustus then goes on with his travels, playing a trick on a horse-courser along the way. Faustus sells him a horse that turns into a heap of straw when ridden into a river. Eventually, Faustus is invited to the court of the Duke of Vanholt, where he performs various feats. The horse-courser shows up there, along with Robin, a man named Dick (Rafe in the A text), and various others who have fallen victim to Faustus's trickery. But Faustus casts spells on them and sends them on their way, to the amusement of the duke and duchess.

As the twenty-four years of his deal with Lucifer come to a close, Faustus begins to dread his impending death. He has Mephastophilis call up Helen of Troy, the famous beauty from the ancient world, and uses her presence to impress a group of scholars. An old man urges Faustus to repent, but Faustus drives him away. Faustus summons Helen again and exclaims rapturously about her beauty. But time is growing short. Faustus tells the scholars about his pact, and they are horror-stricken and resolve to pray for him. On the final night before the expiration of the twenty-four years, Faustus is overcome by fear and remorse. He begs for mercy, but it is too late. At midnight, a host of devils appears and carries his soul off to hell. In the morning, the scholars find Faustus's limbs and decide to hold a funeral for him.

CHARACTER LIST

Faustus   The protagonist. Faustus is a brilliant sixteenth-century scholar from Wittenberg, Germany, whose ambition for knowledge, wealth, and worldly might makes him willing to pay the ultimate price—his soul—to Lucifer in exchange for supernatural powers. Faustus's initial tragic grandeur is diminished by the fact that he never seems completely sure of the decision to forfeit his soul and constantly wavers about whether or not to repent. His ambition is admirable and initially awesome, yet he ultimately lacks a certain inner strength. He is unable to embrace his dark path wholeheartedly but is also unwilling to admit his mistake.

Mephastophilis   A devil whom Faustus summons with his initial magical experiments. Mephastophilis's motivations are ambiguous: on the one hand, his oft-expressed goal is to catch Faustus's soul and carry it off to hell; on the other hand, he actively attempts to dissuade Faustus from making a deal with Lucifer by warning him about the horrors of hell. Mephastophilis is ultimately as tragic a figure as Faustus, with his moving, regretful accounts of what the devils have lost in their eternal separation from God and his repeated reflections on the pain that comes with damnation.

Chorus   A character who stands outside the story, providing narration and commentary. The Chorus was customary in Greek tragedy.

Old Man   An enigmatic figure who appears in the final scene. The old man urges Faustus to repent and to ask God for mercy. He seems to replace the good and evil angels, who, in the first scene, try to influence Faustus's behavior.

Good Angel A spirit that urges Faustus to repent for his pact with Lucifer and return to God. Along with the old man and the bad angel, the good angel represents, in many ways, Faustus's conscience and divided will between good and evil.

Evil Angel A spirit that serves as the counterpart to the good angel and provides Faustus with reasons not to repent for sins against God. The evil angel represents the evil half of Faustus's conscience.

Lucifer The prince of devils, the ruler of hell, and Mephastophilis's master.

Wagner Faustus's servant. Wagner uses his master's books to learn how to summon devils and work magic.

Clown A clown who becomes Wagner's servant. The clown's antics provide comic relief; he is a ridiculous character, and his absurd behavior initially contrasts with Faustus's grandeur. As the play goes on, though, Faustus's behavior comes to resemble that of the clown.

Robin An ostler, or innkeeper, who, like the clown, provides a comic contrast to Faustus. Robin and his friend Rafe learn some basic conjuring, demonstrating that even the least scholarly can possess skill in magic. Marlowe includes Robin and Rafe to illustrate Faustus's degradation as he submits to simple trickery such as theirs.

Rafe An ostler, and a friend of Robin. Rafe appears as Dick (Robin's friend and a clown) in B-text editions of *Doctor Faustus*.

Valdes and Cornelius Two friends of Faustus, both magicians, who teach him the art of black magic.

Horse-courser A horse-trader who buys a horse from Faustus, which vanishes after the horse-courser rides it into the water, leading him to seek revenge.

The Scholars Faustus's colleagues at the University of Wittenberg. Loyal to Faustus, the scholars appear at the beginning and end of the play to express dismay at the turn Faustus's studies have taken, to marvel at his achievements, and then to hear his agonized confession of his pact with Lucifer.

The pope The head of the Roman Catholic Church and a powerful political figure in the Europe of Faustus's day. The pope serves as both a source of amusement for the play's Protestant audience and a symbol of the religious faith that Faustus has rejected.

Emperor Charles V The most powerful monarch in Europe, whose court Faustus visits.

Knight A German nobleman at the emperor's court. The knight is skeptical of Faustus's power, and Faustus makes antlers sprout from his head to teach him a lesson. The knight is further developed and known as Benvolio in B-text versions of *Doctor Faustus*; Benvolio seeks revenge on Faustus and plans to murder him.

Bruno A candidate for the papacy, supported by the emperor. Bruno is captured by the pope and freed by Faustus. Bruno appears only in B-text versions of *Doctor Faustus*.

Duke of Vanholt A German nobleman whom Faustus visits.

Martino and Frederick Friends of Benvolio who reluctantly join his attempt to kill Faustus. Martino and Frederick appear only in B-text versions of *Doctor Faustus*.

Analysis of Major Characters

Faustus

Faustus is the protagonist and tragic hero of Marlowe's play. He is a contradictory character, capable of tremendous eloquence and possessing awesome ambition, yet prone to a strange, almost willful blindness and a willingness to waste powers that he has gained at great cost. When we first meet Faustus, he is just preparing to embark on his career as a magician, and while we already anticipate that things will turn out badly (the Chorus's introduction, if nothing else, prepares us), there is nonetheless a grandeur to Faustus as he contemplates all the marvels that his magical powers will produce. He imagines piling up wealth from the four corners of the globe, reshaping the map of Europe (both politically and physically), and gaining access to every scrap of knowledge about the universe. He is an arrogant, self-aggrandizing man, but his ambitions are so grand that we cannot help being impressed, and we even feel sympathetic toward him. He represents the spirit of the Renaissance, with its rejection of the medieval, God-centered universe, and its embrace of human possibility. Faustus, at least early on in his acquisition of magic, is the personification of possibility.

But Faustus also possesses an obtuseness that becomes apparent during his bargaining sessions with Mephastophilis. Having decided that a pact with the devil is the only way to fulfill his ambitions, Faustus then blinds himself happily to what such a pact actually means. Sometimes he tells himself that hell is not so bad and that one needs only "fortitude"; at other times, even while conversing with Mephastophilis, he remarks to the disbelieving demon that he does not actually believe hell exists. Meanwhile, despite his lack of concern about the prospect of eternal damnation, Faustus is also beset with doubts from the beginning, setting a pattern for the play in which he repeatedly approaches repentance only to pull back at the last moment. Why he fails to repent is unclear: sometimes it seems a matter of pride and continuing ambition, sometimes a conviction that God will not hear his plea. Other times, it seems that Mephastophilis simply bullies him away from repenting.

Bullying Faustus is less difficult than it might seem, because Marlowe, after setting his protagonist up as a grandly tragic figure of sweeping visions and immense ambitions, spends the middle scenes revealing Faustus's true, petty nature. Once Faustus gains his long-desired powers, he does not know what to do with them. Marlowe suggests that this uncertainty stems, in part, from the fact that desire for knowledge leads inexorably toward God, whom Faustus has renounced. But, more generally, absolute power corrupts Faustus: once he can do everything, he no longer wants to do anything. Instead, he traipses around Europe, playing tricks on yokels and performing conjuring acts to impress various heads of state. He uses his incredible gifts for what is essentially trifling entertainment. The fields of possibility narrow gradually, as he visits ever more minor nobles and performs ever more unimportant magic tricks, until the Faustus of the first few scenes is entirely swallowed up in mediocrity. Only in the final scene is Faustus rescued from mediocrity, as the knowledge of his impending doom restores his earlier gift of powerful rhetoric, and he regains his sweeping sense of vision. Now, however, the vision that he sees is of hell looming up to swallow him. Marlowe uses much of his finest poetry to describe Faustus's final hours, during which Faustus's desire for repentance finally wins out, although too late. Still, Faustus is restored to his earlier grandeur in his closing speech, with its hurried rush from idea to idea and its despairing, Renaissance-renouncing last line, "I'll burn my books!" He becomes once again a tragic hero, a great man undone because his ambitions have butted up against the law of God.

MEPHASTOPHILIS

The character of Mephastophilis (spelled Mephistophilis or Mephistopheles by other authors) is one of the first in a long tradition of sympathetic literary devils, which includes figures like John Milton's Satan in Paradise Lost and Johann von Goethe's Mephistophilis in the nineteenth-century poem "Faust." Marlowe's Mephastophilis is particularly interesting because he has mixed motives. On the one hand, from his first appearance he clearly intends to act as an agent of Faustus's damnation. Indeed, he openly admits it, telling Faustus that "when we hear one rack the name of God, / Abjure the Scriptures and his savior Christ, / We fly in hope to get his glorious soul" (3.47–49). It is Mephastophilis who witnesses Faustus's pact with Lucifer, and it is he who, throughout the play, steps in whenever Faustus considers repentance to cajole or threaten him into staying loyal to hell.

Yet there is an odd ambivalence in Mephastophilis. He seeks to damn Faustus, but he himself is damned and speaks freely of the horrors of hell. In a famous passage, when Faustus remarks that the devil seems to be free of hell at a particular moment, Mephastophilis insists,

> [w]hy this is hell, nor am I out of it.
> Think'st thou that I, who saw the face of God,
> And tasted the eternal joys of heaven,
> Am not tormented with ten thousand hells
> In being deprived of everlasting bliss?
> (3.76–80)

Again, when Faustus blithely—and absurdly, given that he is speaking to a demon—declares that he does not believe in hell, Mephastophilis groans and insists that hell is, indeed, real and terrible, as Faustus comes to know soon enough. Before the pact is sealed, Mephastophilis actually warns Faustus against making the deal with Lucifer. In an odd way, one can almost sense that part of Mephastophilis does not want Faustus to make the same mistakes that he made. But, of course, Faustus does so anyway, which makes him and Mephastophilis kindred spirits. It is appropriate that these two figures dominate Marlowe's play, for they are two overly proud spirits doomed to hell.

THEMES, MOTIFS & SYMBOLS

THEMES

Themes are the fundamental and often universal ideas explored in a literary work.

SIN, REDEMPTION, AND DAMNATION

Insofar as *Doctor Faustus* is a Christian play, it deals with the themes at the heart of Christianity's understanding of the world. First, there is the idea of sin, which Christianity defines as acts contrary to the will of God. In making a pact with Lucifer, Faustus commits what is in a sense the ultimate sin: not only does he disobey God, but he consciously and even eagerly renounces obedience to him, choosing instead to swear allegiance to the devil. In a Christian framework, however, even the worst deed can be forgiven through the redemptive power of Jesus Christ, God's son, who, according to Christian belief, died on the cross for humankind's sins. Thus, however terrible Faustus's pact with Lucifer may be, the possibility of redemption is always open to him. All that he needs to do, theoretically, is ask God for forgiveness. The play offers countless moments in which Faustus considers doing just that, urged on by the good angel on his shoulder or by the old man in scene 12—both of whom can be seen either as emissaries of God, personifications of Faustus's conscience, or both.

Each time, Faustus decides to remain loyal to hell rather than seek heaven. In the Christian framework, this turning away from God condemns him to spend an eternity in hell. Only at the end of his life does Faustus desire to repent, and, in the final scene, he cries out to Christ to redeem him. But it is too late for him to repent. In creating this moment in which Faustus is still alive but incapable of being redeemed, Marlowe steps outside the Christian worldview in order to maximize the dramatic power of the final scene. Having inhabited a Christian world for the entire play, Faustus spends his final moments in a slightly different universe, where redemption is no longer possible and where certain sins cannot be forgiven.

THE CONFLICT BETWEEN MEDIEVAL AND RENAISSANCE VALUES

Scholar R.M. Dawkins famously remarked that *Doctor Faustus* tells "the story of a Renaissance man who had to pay the medieval price for being one." While slightly simplistic, this quotation does get at the heart of one of the play's central themes: the clash between the medieval world and the world of the emerging Renaissance. The medieval world placed God at the center of existence and shunted aside man and the natural world. The Renaissance was a movement that began in Italy in the fifteenth century and soon spread throughout Europe, carrying with it a new emphasis on the individual, on classical learning, and on scientific inquiry into the nature of the world. In the medieval academy, theology was the queen of the sciences. In the Renaissance, though, secular matters took center stage.

Faustus, despite being a magician rather than a scientist (a blurred distinction in the sixteenth century), explicitly rejects the medieval model. In his opening speech in scene 1, he goes through every field of scholarship, beginning with logic and proceeding through medicine, law, and theology, quoting an ancient authority for each: Aristotle on logic, Galen on medicine, the Byzantine emperor Justinian on law, and the Bible on religion. In the medieval model, tradition and authority, not individual inquiry, were key. But in this soliloquy, Faustus considers and rejects this medieval way of thinking. He resolves, in full Renaissance spirit, to accept no limits, traditions, or authorities in his quest for knowledge, wealth, and power.

The play's attitude toward the clash between medieval and Renaissance values is ambiguous. Marlowe seems hostile toward the ambitions of Faustus, and, as Dawkins notes, he keeps his tragic hero squarely in the medieval world, where eternal damnation is the price of human pride. Yet Marlowe himself was no pious traditionalist, and it is tempting to see in Faustus—as many readers have—a hero of the new modern world, a world free of God, religion, and the limits that these imposed on humanity. Faustus may pay a medieval price, this reading suggests, but his successors will go further than he and suffer less, as we have in modern times. On the other hand, the disappointment and mediocrity that follow Faustus's pact with the devil, as he descends from grand ambitions to petty conjuring tricks, might suggest a contrasting interpretation. Marlowe may be suggesting that the new, modern spirit, though ambitious and glittering, will lead only to a Faustian dead end.

POWER AS A CORRUPTING INFLUENCE

Early in the play, before he agrees to the pact with Lucifer, Faustus is full of ideas for how to use the power that he seeks. He imagines piling up great wealth, but he also aspires to plumb the mysteries of the universe and to remake the map of Europe. Though they may not be entirely admirable, these plans are ambitious and inspire awe, if not sympathy. They lend a grandeur to Faustus's schemes and make his quest for personal power seem almost heroic, a sense that is reinforced by the eloquence of his early soliloquies.

Once Faustus actually gains the practically limitless power that he so desires, however, his horizons seem to narrow. Everything is possible to him, but his ambition is somehow sapped. Instead of the grand designs that he contemplates early on, he contents himself with performing conjuring tricks for kings and noblemen and takes a strange delight in using his magic to play practical jokes on simple folks. It is not that power has corrupted Faustus by making him evil: indeed, Faustus's behavior after he sells his soul hardly rises to the level of true wickedness. Rather, gaining absolute power corrupts Faustus by making him mediocre and by transforming his boundless ambition into a meaningless delight in petty celebrity.

In the Christian framework of the play, one can argue that true greatness can be achieved only with God's blessing. By cutting himself off from the creator of the universe, Faustus is condemned to mediocrity. He has gained the whole world, but he does not know what to do with it.

THE DIVIDED NATURE OF MAN

Faustus is constantly undecided about whether he should repent and return to God or continue to follow his pact with Lucifer. His internal struggle goes on throughout the play, as part of him of wants to do good and serve God, but part of him (the dominant part, it seems) lusts after the power that Mephastophilis promises. The good angel and the evil angel, both of whom appear at Faustus's shoulder in order to urge him in different directions, symbolize this struggle. While these angels may be intended as an actual pair of supernatural beings, they clearly represent Faustus's divided will, which compels Faustus to commit to Mephastophilis but also to question this commitment continually.

THEMES

MOTIFS

Motifs are recurring structures, contrasts, or literary devices that can help to develop and inform the text's major themes.

MAGIC AND THE SUPERNATURAL

The supernatural pervades *Doctor Faustus*, appearing everywhere in the story. Angels and devils flit about, magic spells are cast, dragons pull chariots (albeit offstage), and even fools like the two ostlers, Robin and Rafe, can learn enough magic to summon demons. Still, it is worth noting that nothing terribly significant is accomplished through magic. Faustus plays tricks on people, conjures up grapes, and explores the cosmos on a dragon, but he does not fundamentally reshape the world. The magic power that Mephastophilis grants him is more like a toy than an awesome, earth-shaking ability. Furthermore, the real drama of the play, despite all the supernatural frills and pyrotechnics, takes place within Faustus's vacillating mind and soul, as he first sells his soul to Lucifer and then considers repenting. In this sense, the magic is almost incidental to the real story of Faustus's struggle with himself, which Marlowe intended not as a fantastical battle but rather as a realistic portrait of a human being with a will divided between good and evil.

PRACTICAL JOKES

Once he gains his awesome powers, Faustus does not use them to do great deeds. Instead, he delights in playing tricks on people: he makes horns sprout from the knight's head and sells the horse-courser an enchanted horse. Such magical practical jokes seem to be Faustus's chief amusement, and Marlowe uses them to illustrate Faustus's decline from a great, prideful scholar into a bored, mediocre magician with no higher ambition than to have a laugh at the expense of a collection of simpletons.

SYMBOLS

Symbols are objects, characters, figures, or colors used to represent abstract ideas or concepts.

BLOOD

Blood plays multiple symbolic roles in the play. When Faustus signs away his soul, he signs in blood, symbolizing the permanent and supernatural nature of this pact. His blood congeals on the page, however, symbolizing, perhaps, his own body's revolt against what he intends to do. Meanwhile, Christ's blood, which Faustus says he sees running across the sky during his terrible last night, symbolizes the sacrifice that Jesus, according to Christian belief, made on the cross; this sacrifice opened the way for humankind to repent its sins and be saved. Faustus, of course, in his proud folly, fails to take this path to salvation.

FAUSTUS'S REJECTION OF THE ANCIENT AUTHORITIES
In scene 1, Faustus goes through a list of the major fields of human knowledge—logic, medicine, law, and theology—and cites for each an ancient authority (Aristotle, Galen, Justinian, and Jerome's Bible, respectively). He then rejects all of these figures in favor of magic. This rejection symbolizes Faustus's break with the medieval world, which prized authority above all else, in favor of a more modern spirit of free inquiry, in which experimentation and innovation trump the assertions of Greek philosophers and the Bible.

THE GOOD ANGEL AND THE EVIL ANGEL
The angels appear at Faustus's shoulder early on in the play—the good angel urging him to repent and serve God, the evil angel urging him to follow his lust for power and serve Lucifer. The two symbolize his divided will, part of which wants to do good and part of which is sunk in sin.

SUMMARY & ANALYSIS

PROLOGUE

SUMMARY: PROLOGUE

The Chorus, a single actor, enters and introduces the plot of the play. It will involve neither love nor war, he tells us, but instead will trace the "form of Faustus' fortunes" (Prologue.8). The Chorus chronicles how Faustus was born to lowly parents in the small town of Rhode, how he came to the town of Wittenberg to live with his kinsmen, and how he was educated at Wittenberg, a famous German university. After earning the title of doctor of divinity, Faustus became famous for his ability to discuss theological matters. The Chorus adds that Faustus is "swollen with cunning" and has begun to practice necromancy, or black magic (Prologue.20). The Prologue concludes by stating that Faustus is seated in his study.

ANALYSIS: PROLOGUE

The Chorus's introduction to the play links Doctor Faustus to the tradition of Greek tragedy, in which a chorus traditionally comments on the action. Although we tend to think of a chorus as a group of people or singers, it can also be composed of only one character. Here, the Chorus not only gives us background information about Faustus's life and education but also explicitly tells us that his swelling pride will lead to his downfall. The story that we are about to see is compared to the Greek myth of Icarus, a boy whose father, Daedalus, gave him wings made out of feathers and beeswax. Icarus did not heed his father's warning and flew too close the sun, causing his wings to melt and sending him plunging to his death. In the same way, the Chorus tells us, Faustus will "mount above his reach" and suffer the consequences (Prologue.21).

The way that the Chorus introduces Faustus, the play's protagonist, is significant, since it reflects a commitment to Renaissance values. The European Renaissance of the fifteenth and sixteenth centuries witnessed a rebirth of interest in classical learning and inaugurated a new emphasis on the individual in painting and literature. In the medieval era that preceded the Renaissance, the focus of scholarship was on God and theology; in the fifteenth and sixteenth centuries, the focus turned toward the study of humankind and the natural world, culminating in the birth of modern science in the work of men like Galileo Galilei and Isaac Newton.

The Prologue locates its drama squarely in the Renaissance world, where humanistic values hold sway. Classical and medieval literature typically focuses on the lives of the great and famous—saints or kings or ancient heroes. But this play, the Chorus insists, will focus not on ancient battles between Rome and Carthage, or on the "courts of kings" or the "pomp of proud audacious deeds" (Prologue.4–5). Instead, we are to witness the life of an ordinary man, born to humble parents. The message is clear: in the new world of the Renaissance, an ordinary man like Faustus, a common-born scholar, is as important as any king or warrior, and his story is just as worthy of being told.

Scene 1

Summary: Scene 1

> *These metaphysics of magicians,*
> *And necromantic books are heavenly!*
> *(See* QUOTATIONS, *p. 41)*

In a long soliloquy, Faustus reflects on the most rewarding type of scholarship. He first considers logic, quoting the Greek philosopher Aristotle, but notes that disputing well seems to be the only goal of logic, and, since Faustus's debating skills are already good, logic is not scholarly enough for him. He considers medicine, quoting the Greek physician Galen, and decides that medicine, with its possibility of achieving miraculous cures, is the most fruitful pursuit—yet he notes that he has achieved great renown as a doctor already and that this fame has not brought him satisfaction. He considers law, quoting the Byzantine emperor Justinian, but dismisses law as too petty, dealing with trivial matters rather than larger ones. Divinity, the study of religion and theology, seems to offer wider vistas, but he quotes from St. Jerome's Bible that all men sin and finds the Bible's assertion that "[t]he reward of sin is death" an unacceptable doctrine. He then dismisses religion and fixes his mind on magic, which, when properly pursued, he believes will make him "a mighty god" (1.62).

Wagner, Faustus's servant, enters as his master finishes speaking. Faustus asks Wagner to bring Valdes and Cornelius, Faustus's friends, to help him learn the art of magic. While they are on their way, a good angel and an evil angel visit Faustus. The good angel urges him to set aside his book of magic and read the Scriptures instead; the evil angel encourages him to go forward in his pursuit of the black arts. After they vanish, it is clear that Faustus is going to heed the evil spirit, since he exults at the great powers that the magical arts will bring him. Faustus imagines sending spirits to the end of the world to fetch him jewels and delicacies, having them teach him secret knowledge, and using magic to make himself king of all Germany.

Valdes and Cornelius appear, and Faustus greets them, declaring that he has set aside all other forms of learning in favor of magic. They agree to teach Faustus the principles of the dark arts and describe the wondrous powers that will be his if he remains committed during his quest to learn magic. Cornelius tells him that "[t]he miracles that magic will perform / Will make thee vow to study nothing else" (1.136–137). Valdes lists a number of texts that Faustus should read, and the two friends promise to help him become better at magic than even they are. Faustus invites them to dine with him, and they exit.

ANALYSIS: SCENE 1

The scene now shifts to Faustus's study, and Faustus's opening speech about the various fields of scholarship reflects the academic setting of the scene. In proceeding through the various intellectual disciplines and citing authorities for each, he is following the dictates of medieval scholarship, which held that learning was based on the authority of the wise rather than on experimentation and new ideas. This soliloquy, then, marks Faustus's rejection of this medieval model, as he sets aside each of the old authorities and resolves to strike out on his own in his quest to become powerful through magic.

As is true throughout the play, however, Marlowe uses Faustus's own words to expose Faustus's blind spots. In his initial speech, for example, Faustus establishes a hierarchy of disciplines by showing which are nobler than others. He does not want merely to protect men's bodies through medicine, nor does he want to protect their property through law. He wants higher things, and so he proceeds on to religion. There, he quotes selectively from the New Testament, picking out only those passages that make Christianity appear in a negative light. He reads that "[t]he reward of sin is death," and that "[i]f we say we that we have no sin, / We deceive ourselves, and there is no truth in us" (1.40–43). The second of these lines comes from the first book of John, but Faustus neglects to read the very next line, which states, "If we confess our sins, [God] is faithful and just to forgive us our sins, and to cleanse us from all unrighteousness" (1 John 1:9). Thus, through selective quoting, Faustus makes it seem as though religion promises only death and not forgiveness, and so he easily rejects religion with a fatalistic "What will be, shall be! Divinity, adieu!" (1.48). Meanwhile, he uses religious language—as he does throughout the play—to describe the dark world of necromancy that he enters. "These metaphysics of magicians / And necromantic books are heavenly" (1.49–50), he declares without out a trace of irony. Having gone upward from medicine and law to theology, he envisions magic and necromancy as the crowning discipline, even though by most standards it would be the least noble.

Faustus is not a villain, though; he is a tragic hero, a protagonist whose character flaws lead to his downfall. Marlowe imbues him with tragic grandeur in these early scenes. The logic he uses to reject religion may be flawed, but there is something impressive in the breadth of his ambition, even if he pursues it through diabolical means. In Faustus's long speech after the two angels have whispered in his ears, his rhetoric outlines the modern quest for control over nature (albeit through magic rather than through science) in glowing, inspiring language. He offers a long list of impressive goals, including the acquisition of knowledge, wealth, and political power, that he believes he will achieve once he has mastered the dark arts. While the reader or playgoer is not expected to approve of his quest, his ambitions are impressive, to say the least. Later, the actual uses to which he puts his magical powers are disappointing and tawdry. For now, however, Faustus's dreams inspire wonder.

SCENES 2–4

SUMMARY: SCENE 2

Two scholars come to see Faustus. Wagner makes jokes at their expense and then tells them that Faustus is meeting with Valdes and Cornelius. Aware that Valdes and Cornelius are infamous for their involvement in the black arts, the scholars leave with heavy hearts, fearing that Faustus may also be falling into "that damned art" as well (2.29).

SUMMARY: SCENE 3

> *Think'st thou that I, who saw the face of God,*
> *And tasted the eternal joys of heaven,*
> *Am not tormented with ten thousand hells*
> *In being deprived of everlasting bliss?*
>
> *(See* QUOTATIONS, *p. 42)*

That night, Faustus stands in a magical circle marked with various signs and words, and he chants in Latin. Four devils and Lucifer, the ruler of hell, watch him from the shadows. Faustus renounces heaven and God, swears allegiance to hell, and demands that Mephastophilis rise to serve him. The devil Mephastophilis then appears before Faustus, who commands him to depart and return dressed as a Franciscan friar, since "[t]hat holy shape becomes a devil best" (3.26). Mephastophilis vanishes, and Faustus remarks on his obedience. Mephastophilis then reappears, dressed as a monk, and asks Faustus what he desires. Faustus demands his obedience, but Mephastophilis says that he is Lucifer's servant and can obey only Lucifer. He adds that he came because he heard Faustus deny obedience to God and hoped to capture his soul.

Faustus quizzes Mephastophilis about Lucifer and hell and learns that Lucifer and all his devils were once angels who rebelled against God and have been damned to hell forever. Faustus points out that Mephastophilis is not in hell now but on earth; Mephastophilis insists, however, that he and his fellow demons are always in hell, even when they are on earth, because being deprived of the presence of God, which they once enjoyed, is hell enough. Faustus dismisses this sentiment as a lack of fortitude on Mephastophilis's part and then declares that he will offer his soul to Lucifer in return for twenty-four years of Mephastophilis's service. Mephastophilis agrees to take this offer to his master and departs. Left alone, Faustus remarks that if he had "as many souls as there be stars," he would offer them all to hell in return for the kind of power that Mephastophilis offers him (3.102). He eagerly awaits Mephastophilis's return.

SUMMARY: SCENE 4

Wagner converses with a clown and tries to persuade him to become his servant for seven years. The clown is poor, and Wagner jokes that he would probably sell his soul to the devil for a shoulder of mutton; the clown answers that it would have to be well-seasoned mutton. After first agreeing to be Wagner's servant, however, the clown abruptly changes his mind. Wagner threatens to cast a spell on him, and he then conjures up two devils, who he says will carry the clown away to hell unless he becomes Wagner's servant. Seeing the devils, the clown becomes terrified and agrees to Wagner's demands. After Wagner dismisses the devils, the clown asks his new master if he can learn to conjure as well, and Wagner promises to teach him how to turn himself into any kind of animal—but he insists on being called "Master Wagner."

ANALYSIS: SCENES 2–4

Having learned the necessary arts from Cornelius and Valdes, Faustus now takes the first step toward selling his soul when he conjures up a devil. One of the central questions in the play is whether Faustus damns himself entirely on his own or whether the princes of hell somehow entrap him. In scene 3, as Faustus makes the magical marks and chants the magical words that summon Mephastophilis, he is watched by Lucifer and four lesser devils, suggesting that hell is waiting for him to make the first move before pouncing on him. Mephastophilis echoes this idea when he insists that he came to Faustus of his own accord when he heard Faustus curse God and forswear heaven, hoping that Faustus's soul was available for the taking. But while the demons may be active agents eagerly seeking to seize Faustus's soul, Faustus himself makes the first move. Neither Mephastophilis nor Lucifer forces him to do anything against his will.

Indeed, if anything, Mephastophilis seems far less eager to make the bargain than Faustus himself. He willingly tells Faustus that his master, Lucifer, is less powerful than God, having been thrown "by aspiring pride and insolence, / ... from the face of heaven" (3.67–68). Furthermore, Mephastophilis offers a powerful portrait of hell that seems to warn against any pact with Lucifer. When Faustus asks him how it is that he is allowed to leave hell in order to come to earth, Mephastophilis famously says:

> Why this is hell, nor am I out of it.
> Think'st thou that I, who saw the face of God,
> And tasted the eternal joys of heaven,
> Am not tormented with ten thousand hells
> In being deprived of everlasting bliss?
> (3.76–80)

Mephastophilis exposes the horrors of his own experience as if offering sage guidance to Faustus. His honesty in mentioning the "ten thousand hells" that torment him shines a negative light on the action of committing one's soul to Lucifer. Indeed, Mephastophilis even tells Faustus to abandon his "frivolous demands" (3.81).

But Faustus refuses to leave his desires. Instead, he exhibits the blindness that serves as one of his defining characteristics throughout the play. Faustus sees the world as he wants to see it rather than as it is. This shunning of reality is symbolized by his insistence that Mephastophilis, who is presumably hideous, reappear as a Franciscan friar. In part, this episode is a dig at Catholicism, pitched at Marlowe's fiercely Protestant English audience, but it also shows to what lengths Faustus will go in order to mitigate the horrors of hell. He sees the devil's true shape, but rather than flee in terror he tells Mephastophilis to change his appearance, which makes looking upon him easier. Again, when Mephastophilis has finished telling him of the horrors of hell and urging him not to sell his soul, Faustus blithely dismisses what Mephastophilis has said, accusing him of lacking "manly fortitude" (3.85). There is a desperate naïveté to Faustus's approach to the demonic: he cannot seem to accept that hell is really as bad as it seems, which propels him forward into darkness.

The antics of Wagner and the clown provide a comic counterpoint to the Faustus-Mephastophilis scenes. The clown jokes that he would sell his soul to the devil for a well-seasoned shoulder of mutton, and Wagner uses his newly gained conjuring skill to frighten the clown into serving him. Like Faustus, these clownish characters (whose scenes are so different from the rest of the play that some writers have suggested that they were written by a collaborator rather than by Marlowe himself) use magic to summon demons. But where Faustus is grand and ambitious and tragic, they are low and common and absurd, seeking mutton and the ability to turn into a mouse or a rat rather than world power or fantastic wealth. As the play progresses, though, Faustus's grandeur diminishes, and he sinks down toward the level of the clowns, suggesting that degradation precedes damnation.

SCENES 5–6

SUMMARY: SCENE 5

> *Think'st thou that Faustus is so fond to imagine*
> *That after this life there is any pain?*
> *Tush, these are trifles and mere old wives' tales.*
> *(See QUOTATIONS, p. 43)*

Faustus begins to waver in his conviction to sell his soul. The good angel tells him to abandon his plan and "think of heaven, and heavenly things," but he dismisses the good angel's words, saying that God does not love him (5.20). The good and evil angels make another appearance, with the good one again urging Faustus to think of heaven, but the evil angel convinces him that the wealth he can gain through his deal with the devil is worth the cost. Faustus then calls back Mephastophilis, who tells him that Lucifer has accepted his offer of his soul in exchange for twenty-four years of service. Faustus asks Mephastophilis why Lucifer wants his soul, and Mephastophilis tells him that Lucifer seeks to enlarge his kingdom and make humans suffer even as he suffers.

Faustus decides to make the bargain, and he stabs his arm in order to write the deed in blood. However, when he tries to write the deed his blood congeals, making writing impossible. Mephastophilis goes to fetch fire in order to loosen the blood, and, while he is gone, Faustus endures another bout of indecision, as he wonders if his own blood is attempting to warn him not to sell his soul. When Mephastophilis returns, Faustus signs the deed and then discovers an inscription on his arm that reads "Homo fuge," Latin for "O man, fly" (5.77). While Faustus wonders where he should fly Mephastophilis presents a group of devils, who cover Faustus with crowns and rich garments. Faustus puts aside his doubts. He hands over the deed, which promises his body and soul to Lucifer in exchange for twenty-four years of constant service from Mephastophilis.

After he turns in the deed, Faustus asks his new servant where hell is located, and Mephastophilis says that it has no exact location but exists everywhere. He continues explaining, saying that hell is everywhere that the damned are cut off from God eternally. Faustus remarks that he thinks hell is a myth. At Faustus's request for a wife, Mephastophilis offers Faustus a she-devil, but Faustus refuses. Mephastophilis then gives him a book of magic spells and tells him to read it carefully.

Faustus once again wavers and leans toward repentance as he contemplates the wonders of heaven from which he has cut himself off. The good and evil angels appear again, and Faustus realizes that "[m]y heart's so hardened I cannot repent!" (5.196). He then begins to ask Mephastophilis questions about the planets and the heavens. Mephastophilis answers all his queries willingly, until Faustus asks who made the world. Mephastophilis refuses to reply because the answer is "against our kingdom"; when Faustus presses him, Mephastophilis departs angrily (5.247). Faustus then turns his mind to God, and again he wonders if it is too late for him to repent. The good and evil angels enter once more, and the good angel says it is never too late for Faustus to repent. Faustus begins to appeal to Christ for mercy, but then Lucifer, Belzebub (another devil), and Mephastophilis enter. They tell Faustus to stop thinking of God and then present a show of the Seven Deadly Sins. Each sin—Pride, Covetousness, Envy, Wrath, Gluttony, Sloth, and finally Lechery—appears before Faustus and makes a brief speech. The sight of the sins delights Faustus's soul, and he asks to see hell. Lucifer promises to take him there that night. For the meantime he gives Faustus a book that teaches him how to change his shape.

SUMMARY: SCENE 6

Meanwhile, Robin, a stablehand, has found one of Faustus's conjuring books, and he is trying to learn the spells. He calls in an innkeeper named Rafe, and the two go to a bar together, where Robin promises to conjure up any kind of wine that Rafe desires.

ANALYSIS: SCENES 5–6

Even as he seals the bargain that promises his soul to hell, Faustus is repeatedly filled with misgivings, which are bluntly symbolized in the verbal duels between the good and evil angels. His body seems to rebel against the choices that he has made—his blood congeals, for example, preventing him from signing the compact, and a written warning telling him to fly away appears on his arm. Sometimes Faustus seems to understand the gravity of what he is doing: when Lucifer, Belzebub, and Mephastophilis appear to him, for example, he becomes suddenly afraid and exclaims, "O Faustus, they are come to fetch thy soul!" (5.264). Despite this awareness, however, Faustus is unable to commit to good.

Amid all these signs, Faustus repeatedly considers repenting but each time decides against it. Sometimes it is the lure of knowledge and riches that prevents him from turning to God, but other times it seems to be his conviction—encouraged by the bad angel and Mephastophilis—that it is already too late for him, a conviction that persists throughout the play. He believes that God does not love him and that if he were to fly away to God, as the inscription on his arm seems to advise him to do, God would cast him down to hell. When Faustus appeals to Christ to save his soul, Lucifer declares that "Christ cannot save thy soul, for he is just," and orders Faustus to cease thinking about God and think only of the devil (5.260). Faustus's sense that he is already damned can be traced back to his earlier misreading of the New Testament to say that anyone who sins will be damned eternally—ignoring the verses that offer the hope of repentance.

At the same time, though, Faustus's earlier blindness persists. We can see it in his delighted reaction to the appalling personifications of the Seven Deadly Sins, which he treats as sources of entertainment rather than of moral warning. Meanwhile, his willingness to dismiss the pains of hell continues, as he tells Mephastophilis that "I think hell's a fable / . . . / Tush, these are trifles and mere old wives' tales" (5.126–135). These are the words of rationalism or even atheism—both odd ideologies for Faustus to espouse, given that he is summoning devils. But Faustus's real mistake is to misinterpret what Mephastophilis tells him about hell. Faustus takes Mephastophilis's statement that hell is everywhere for him because he is separated eternally from God to mean that hell will be merely a continuation of his earthly existence. He thinks that he is already separated from God permanently and reasons that hell cannot be any worse.

Once Faustus has signed away his soul, his cosmos seems to become inverted, with Lucifer taking the place of God and blasphemy replacing piety. After Faustus has signed his deed, he swears by Lucifer rather than God: "Ay, take it; and the devil give thee good on't" (5.112). His rejection of God is also evident when he says, "Consummatum est," meaning "it is finished," which were Christ's dying words on the cross (5.74). Even Faustus's arm stabbing alludes to the stigmata, or wounds, of the crucified Christ.

Meanwhile, the limits of the demonic gifts that Faustus has been given begin to emerge. He is given the gift of knowledge, and Mephastophilis willingly tells him the secrets of astronomy, but when Faustus asks who created the world, Mephastophilis refuses to answer. The symbolism is clear: all the worldly knowledge that Faustus has so strongly desired points inexorably upward, toward God. The central irony, of course, is that the pact he has made completely detaches him from God. With access to higher things thus closed off, Faustus has nowhere to go but down.

CHORUS 2–SCENE 8

SUMMARY: CHORUS 2

Wagner takes the stage and describes how Faustus traveled through the heavens on a chariot pulled by dragons in order to learn the secrets of astronomy. Wagner tells us that Faustus is now traveling to measure the coasts and kingdoms of the world and that his travels will take him to Rome.

SUMMARY: SCENE 7

Faustus appears, recounting to Mephastophilis his travels throughout Europe—first from Germany to France and then on to Italy. He asks Mephastophilis if they have arrived in Rome, whose monuments he greatly desires to see, and Mephastophilis replies that they are in the pope's privy chamber. It is a day of feasting in Rome, to celebrate the pope's victories, and Faustus and Mephastophilis agree to use their powers to play tricks on the pope.

> NOTE: The events described in the next two paragraphs occur only in the B text of Doctor Faustus, in Act III, scene i. The A text omits the events described in the next two paragraphs but resumes with the events described immediately after them.

As Faustus and Mephastophilis watch, the pope comes in with his attendants and a prisoner, Bruno, who had attempted to become pope with the backing of the German emperor. While the pope declares that he will depose the emperor and forces Bruno to swear allegiance to him, Faustus and Mephastophilis disguise themselves as cardinals and come before the pope. The pope gives Bruno to them, telling them to carry him off to prison; instead, they give him a fast horse and send him back to Germany.

Later, the pope confronts the two cardinals whom Faustus and Mephastophilis have impersonated. When the cardinals say that they never were given custody of Bruno, the pope sends them to the dungeon. Faustus and Mephastophilis, both invisible, watch the proceedings and chuckle. The pope and his attendants then sit down to dinner. During the meal, Faustus and Mephastophilis make themselves invisible and curse noisily and then snatch dishes and food as they are passed around the table. The churchmen suspect that there is some ghost in the room, and the pope begins to cross himself, much to the dismay of Faustus and Mephastophilis. Faustus boxes the pope's ear, and the pope and all his attendants run away. A group of friars enters, and they sing a dirge damning the unknown spirit that has disrupted the meal. Mephastophilis and Faustus beat the friars, fling fireworks among them, and flee.

SUMMARY: SCENE 8
Robin the ostler, or stablehand, and his friend Rafe have stolen a cup from a tavern. They are pursued by a vintner (or wine-maker), who demands that they return the cup. They claim not to have it, and then Robin conjures up Mephastophilis, which makes the vintner flee. Mephastophilis is not pleased to have been summoned for a prank, and he threatens to turn the two into an ape and a dog. The two friends treat what they have done as a joke, and Mephastophilis leaves in a fury, saying that he will go to join Faustus in Turkey.

ANALYSIS: CHORUS 2–SCENE 8
The scenes in Rome are preceded by Wagner's account, in the second chorus, of how Faustus traveled through the heavens studying astronomy. This feat is easily the most impressive that Faustus performs in the entire play, since his magical abilities seem more and more like cheap conjured tricks as the play progresses. Meanwhile, his interests also diminish in importance from astronomy, the study of the heavens, to cosmography, the study of the earth. He even begins to meddle in political matters in the assistance he gives Bruno (in the B text only). By the end of the play, his chief interests are playing practical jokes and producing impressive illusions for nobles—a far cry from the ambitious pursuits that he outlines in scene 1.

Faustus's interactions with the pope and his courtiers offer another send-up of the Catholic Church. The pope's grasping ambition and desire for worldly power would have played into late-sixteenth-century English stereotypes. By having the invisible Faustus box the papal ears and disrupt the papal banquet, Marlowe makes a laughingstock out of the head of the Catholic Church. Yet the absurdity of the scene coexists with a suggestion that, ridiculous as they are, the pope and his attendants do possess some kind of divinely sanctioned power, which makes them symbols of Christianity and sets their piety in opposition to Faustus's devil-inspired magic. When the pope and his monks begin to rain curses on their invisible tormentors, Faustus and Mephastophilis seem to fear the power that their words invoke. Mephastophilis says, "[W]e shall be cursed with bell, / book, and candle" (7.81–82). The fear-imposing power these religious symbols have over Mephastophilis suggests that God remains stronger than the devil and that perhaps Faustus could still be saved, if he repented in spite of everything. Faustus's reply—"Bell, book and candle; candle, book, and bell / Forward and backward, to curse Faustus to hell"—is fraught with foreshadowing (7.83–84). Hell, of course, is exactly where Faustus is "curse[d]" to go, but through his own folly and not the curses of monks or the pope.

The absurd behavior of Robin and Rafe, meanwhile, once again contrasts with Faustus's relationship to the diabolical. Robin and Rafe conjure up Mephastophilis in order to scare off a vintner, and even when he threatens to turn them into animals (or actually does so temporarily—the text is unclear on this matter), they treat it as a great joke. Yet the contrast between Faustus on the one hand and the ostlers and the clown on the other, the high and the low, is not so great as it is originally, since Faustus too has begun using magic in pursuit of practical jokes, like boxing the pope's ear. Such foolishness is quite a step down for a man who earlier speaks of using his magic to become ruler of Germany. Although Faustus does step into the political realm when he frees Bruno and sends him back to Germany, this action seems to be carried out as part of the cruel practical joke on the pope, not as part of any real political pursuit. The degradation of Faustus's initially heroic aims continues as the play proceeds, with Faustus coming to resemble a clown more and more.

Chorus 3–Scene 9

Summary: Chorus 3

The Chorus enters to inform us that Faustus has returned home to Germany and developed his fame by explaining what he learned during the course of his journey. The German emperor, Charles V, has heard of Faustus and invited him to his palace, where we next encounter him.

SUMMARY: SCENE 9

> NOTE: The events described in the first two paragraphs of
> this summary occur only in the B text of Doctor Faustus, in
> Act IV, scenes i–ii. The A text omits the events described in
> the first two paragraphs but resumes with the events
> described immediately after them.

At the court of the emperor, two gentlemen, Martino and Frederick,
discuss the imminent arrival of Bruno and Faustus. Martino
remarks that Faustus has promised to conjure up Alexander the
Great, the famous conqueror. The two of them wake another gentle-
man, Benvolio, and tell him to come down and see the new arrivals,
but Benvolio declares that he would rather watch the action from
his window, because he has a hangover.

Faustus comes before the emperor, who thanks him for having
freed Bruno from the clutches of the pope. Faustus acknowledges
the gratitude and then says that he stands ready to fulfill any wish
that the emperor might have. Benvolio, watching from above,
remarks to himself that Faustus looks nothing like what he would
expect a conjurer to look like.

The emperor tells Faustus that he would like to see Alexander the
Great and his lover. Faustus tells him that he cannot produce their
actual bodies but can create spirits resembling them. A knight
present in the court (Benvolio in the B text) is skeptical, and asserts
that it is as untrue that Faustus can perform this feat as that the god-
dess Diana has transformed the knight into a stag.

Before the eyes of the court, Faustus creates a vision of Alexander
embracing his lover (in the B text, Alexander's great rival, the Per-
sian king Darius, also appears; Alexander defeats Darius and then,
along with his lover, salutes the emperor). Faustus conjures a pair of
antlers onto the head of the knight (again, Benvolio in the B text).
The knight pleads for mercy, and the emperor entreats Faustus to
remove the horns. Faustus complies, warning Benvolio to have
more respect for scholars in the future.

> NOTE: The following scenes do not appear in the A text of
> Doctor Faustus. The summary below corresponds to Act IV,
> scenes iii–iv, in the B text.

With his friends Martino and Frederick and a group of soldiers, Benvolio plots an attack against Faustus. His friends try to dissuade him, but he is so furious at the damage done to his reputation that he will not listen to reason. They resolve to ambush Faustus as he leaves the court of the emperor and to take the treasures that the emperor has given Faustus. Frederick goes out with the soldiers to scout and returns with word that Faustus is coming toward them and that he is alone. When Faustus enters, Benvolio stabs him and cuts off his head. He and his friends rejoice, and they plan the further indignities that they will visit on Faustus's corpse. But then Faustus rises with his head restored. Faustus tells them that they are fools, since his life belongs to Mephastophilis and cannot be taken by anyone else. He summons Mephastophilis, who arrives with a group of lesser devils, and orders the devils to carry his attackers off to hell. Then, reconsidering, he orders them instead to punish Benvolio and his friends by dragging them through thorns and hurling them off of cliffs, so that the world will see what happens to people who attack Faustus. As the men and devils leave, the soldiers come in, and Faustus summons up another clutch of demons to drive them off.

Benvolio, Frederick, and Martino reappear. They are bruised and bloody from having been chased and harried by the devils, and all three of them now have horns sprouting from their heads. They greet one another unhappily, express horror at the fate that has befallen them, and agree to conceal themselves in a castle rather than face the scorn of the world.

ANALYSIS: CHORUS 3–SCENE 9

Twenty-four years pass between Faustus's pact with Lucifer and the end of the play. Yet, for us, these decades sweep by remarkably quickly. We see only three main events from the twenty-four years: Faustus's visits to Rome, to the emperor's court, and then to the Duke of Vanholt in scene 11. While the Chorus assures us that Faustus visits many other places and learns many other things that we are not shown, we are still left with the sense that Faustus's life is being accelerated at a speed that strains belief. But Marlowe uses this acceleration to his advantage. By making the years pass so swiftly, the play makes us feel what Faustus himself must feel—namely, that his too-short lifetime is slipping away from him and his ultimate, hellish fate is drawing ever closer. In the world of the play, twenty-four years seems long when Faustus makes the pact, but both he and we come to realize that it passes rapidly.

Meanwhile, the use to which Faustus puts his powers is unim
pressive. In Rome, he and Mephastophilis box the pope's ears and
disrupt a dinner party. At the court of Emperor Charles V (who
ruled a vast stretch of territory in the sixteenth century, including
Germany, Austria, and Spain), he essentially performs conjuring
tricks to entertain the monarch. Before he makes the pact with Lucifer, Faustus speaks of rearranging the geography of Europe or even
making himself emperor of Germany. Now, though, his sights are
set considerably lower. His involvement in the political realm
extends only to freeing Bruno, Charles's candidate to be pope. Even
this action (which occurs only in the B text) seems largely a lark,
without any larger political goals behind it. Instead, Faustus occupies his energies summoning up Alexander the Great, the heroic
Macedonian conqueror. This trick would be extremely impressive,
except that Faustus tells the emperor that "it is not in my ability to
present / before your eyes the true substantial bodies of those two
deceased / princes" (9.39–41). In other words, all of Mephastophilis's power can, in Faustus's hands, produce only impressive illusions. Nothing of substance emerges from Faustus's magic, in this
scene or anywhere in the play, and the man who earlier boasts that
he will divert the River Rhine and reshape the map of Europe now
occupies himself with revenging a petty insult by placing horns on
the head of the foolish knight.

The B-text scene outside the emperor's court, in which Benvolio
and his friends try to kill Faustus, is utterly devoid of suspense, since
we know that Faustus is too powerful to be murdered by a gang of
incompetent noblemen. Still, Faustus's way of dealing with the
threat is telling: he plays a kind of practical joke, making the noblemen think that they have cut off his head, only to come back to life
and send a collection of devils to hound them. With all the power of
hell behind him, he takes pleasure in sending Mephastophilis out to
hunt down a collection of fools who pose no threat to him and
insists that the devils disgrace the men publicly, so that everyone will
see what happens to those who threaten him. This command shows
a hint of Faustus's old pride, which is so impressive early in the play;
now, though, Faustus is entirely concerned with his reputation as a
fearsome wizard and not with any higher goals. Traipsing from
court to court, doing tricks for royals, Faustus has become a kind of
sixteenth-century celebrity, more concerned with his public image
than with the dreams of greatness that earlier animate him.

SCENES 10–11

SUMMARY: SCENE 10

Faustus, meanwhile, meets a horse-courser and sells him his horse. Faustus gives the horse-courser a good price but warns him not to ride the horse into the water. Faustus begins to reflect on the pending expiration of his contract with Lucifer and falls asleep. The horse-courser reappears, sopping wet, complaining that when he rode his horse into a stream it turned into a heap of straw. He decides to get his money back and tries to wake Faustus by hollering in his ear. He then pulls on Faustus's leg when Faustus will not wake. The leg breaks off, and Faustus wakes up, screaming bloody murder. The horse-courser takes the leg and runs off. Meanwhile, Faustus's leg is immediately restored, and he laughs at the joke that he has played. Wagner then enters and tells Faustus that the Duke of Vanholt has summoned him. Faustus agrees to go, and they depart together.

Note: The following scene does not appear in the A text of Doctor Faustus. The summary below corresponds to Act IV, scene vi, in the B text.

Robin and Rafe have stopped for a drink in a tavern. They listen as a carter, or wagon-driver, and the horse-courser discuss Faustus. The carter explains that Faustus stopped him on the road and asked to buy some hay to eat. The carter agreed to sell him all he could eat for three farthings, and Faustus proceeded to eat the entire wagon-load of hay. The horse-courser tells his own story, adding that he took Faustus's leg as revenge and that he is keeping it at his home. Robin declares that he intends to seek out Faustus, but only after he has a few more drinks.

SUMMARY: SCENE 11

At the court of the Duke of Vanholt, Faustus's skill at conjuring up beautiful illusions wins the duke's favor. Faustus comments that the duchess has not seemed to enjoy the show and asks her what she would like. She tells him she would like a dish of ripe grapes, and Faustus has Mephastophilis bring her some grapes. (In the B text of *Doctor Faustus*, Robin, Dick, the carter, the horse-courser, and the hostess from the tavern burst in at this moment. They confront Faustus, and the horse-courser begins making jokes about what he assumes is Faustus's wooden leg. Faustus then shows them his leg, which is whole and healthy, and they are amazed. Each then launches into a complaint about Faustus's treatment of him, but Faustus uses magical charms to make them silent, and they depart.) The duke and duchess are much pleased with Faustus's display, and they promise to reward Faustus greatly.

ANALYSIS: SCENES 10–11

Faustus's downward spiral, from tragic greatness to self-indulgent mediocrity, continues in these scenes. He continues his journey from court to court, arriving this time at Vanholt, a minor German duchy, to visit the duke and duchess. Over the course of the play we see Faustus go from the seat of the pope to the court of the emperor to the court of a minor nobleman. The power and importance of his hosts decreases from scene to scene, just as Faustus's feats of magic grow ever more unimpressive. Just after he seals his pact with Mephastophilis, Faustus soars through the heavens on a chariot pulled by dragons to learn the secrets of astronomy; now, however, he is reduced to playing pointless tricks on the horse-courser and fetching out-of-season grapes to impress a bored noblewoman. Even his antagonists have grown increasingly ridiculous. In Rome, he faces the curses of the pope and his monks, which are strong enough to give even Mephastophilis pause; at the emperor's court, Faustus is opposed by a collection of noblemen who are brave, if unintelligent. At Vanholt, though, he faces down an absurd collection of comical rogues, and the worst of it is that Faustus seems to have become one of them, a clown among clowns, taking pleasure in using his unlimited power to perform practical jokes and cast simple charms.

Selling one's soul for power and glory may be foolish or wicked, but at least there is grandeur to the idea of it. Marlowe's Faustus, however, has lost his hold on that doomed grandeur and has become pathetic. The meaning of his decline is ambiguous: perhaps part of the nature of a pact with Lucifer is that one cannot gain all that one hopes to gain from it. Or perhaps Marlowe is criticizing worldly ambition and, by extension, the entire modern project of the Renaissance, which pushed God to one side and sought mastery over nature and society. Along the lines of this interpretation, it seems that in Marlowe's worldview the desire for complete knowledge about the world and power over it can ultimately be reduced to fetching grapes for the Duchess of Vanholt—in other words, to nothing.

Earlier in the play, when Faustus queries Mephastophilis about the nature of the world, Faustus sees his desire for knowledge reach a dead end at God, whose power he denies in favor of Lucifer.

Knowledge of God is against Lucifer's kingdom, according to Mephastophilis. But if the pursuit of knowledge leads inexorably to God, Marlowe suggests, then a man like Faustus, who tries to live without God, can ultimately go nowhere but down, into mediocrity.

There is no sign that Faustus himself is aware of the gulf between his earlier ambitions and his current state. He seems to take joy in his petty amusements, laughing uproariously when he confounds the horse-courser and leaping at the chance to visit the Duke of Vanholt. Still, his impending doom begins to weigh upon him. As he sits down to fall asleep, he remarks, "What art thou, Faustus, but a man condemned to die?" (10.24). Yet, at this moment at least, he seems convinced that he will repent at the last minute and be saved—a significant change from his earlier attitude, when he either denies the existence of hell or assumes that damnation is inescapable. "Christ did call the thief upon the cross," he comforts himself, referring to the New Testament story of the thief who was crucified alongside Jesus Christ, repented for his sins, and was promised a place in paradise (10.28). That he compares himself to this figure shows that Faustus assumes that he can wait until the last moment and still escape hell. In other words, he wants to renounce Mephastophilis, but not just yet. We can easily anticipate that his willingness to delay will prove fatal.

Chorus 4–Epilogue

Summary: Chorus 4

Wagner announces that Faustus must be about to die because he has given Wagner all of his wealth. But he remains unsure, since Faustus is not acting like a dying man—rather, he is out carousing with scholars.

Summary: Scene 12

> *Sweet Helen, make me immortal with a kiss:*
> *Her lips sucks forth my soul, see where it flies!*
> *Come Helen, come, give me my soul again.*
> *Here will I dwell, for heaven be in these lips,*
> *And all is dross that is not Helena!*
>
> *(See* QUOTATIONS, *p. 44)*

Faustus enters with some of the scholars. One of them asks Faustus if he can produce Helen of Greece (also known as Helen of Troy), who they have decided was "the admirablest lady / that ever lived" (12.3–4). Faustus agrees to produce her, and gives the order to Mephastophilis: immediately, Helen herself crosses the stage, to the delight of the scholars.

The scholars leave, and an old man enters and tries to persuade Faustus to repent. Faustus becomes distraught, and Mephastophilis hands him a dagger. However, the old man persuades him to appeal to God for mercy, saying, "I see an angel hovers o'er thy head / And with a vial full of precious grace / Offers to pour the same into thy soul!" (12.44–46). Once the old man leaves, Mephastophilis threatens to shred Faustus to pieces if he does not reconfirm his vow to Lucifer. Faustus complies, sealing his vow by once again stabbing his arm and inscribing it in blood. He asks Mephastophilis to punish the old man for trying to dissuade him from continuing in Lucifer's service; Mephastophilis says that he cannot touch the old man's soul but that he will scourge his body. Faustus then asks Mephastophilis to let him see Helen again. Helen enters, and Faustus makes a great speech about her beauty and kisses her.

SUMMARY: SCENE 13

> Now hast thou but one bare hour to live,
> And then thou must be damned perpetually.
> Ugly hell gape not! Come not, Lucifer!
> I'll burn my books—ah, Mephastophilis!
>
> (See QUOTATIONS, p. 45)

The final night of Faustus's life has come, and he tells the scholars of the deal he has made with Lucifer. They are horrified and ask what they can do to save him, but he tells them that there is nothing to be done. Reluctantly, they leave to pray for Faustus. A vision of hell opens before Faustus's horrified eyes as the clock strikes eleven. The last hour passes by quickly, and Faustus exhorts the clocks to slow and time to stop, so that he might live a little longer and have a chance to repent. He then begs God to reduce his time in hell to a thousand years or a hundred thousand years, so long as he is eventually saved. He wishes that he were a beast and would simply cease to exist when he dies instead of face damnation. He curses his parents and himself, and the clock strikes midnight. Devils enter and carry Faustus away as he screams, "Ugly hell gape not! Come not, Lucifer! / I'll burn my books—ah, Mephastophilis!" (13.112–113).

Summary: Epilogue

The Chorus enters and warns the wise "[o]nly to wonder at unlawful things" and not to trade their souls for forbidden knowledge (Epilogue.6).

Analysis: Chorus 4–Epilogue

The final scenes contain some of the most noteworthy speeches in the play, especially Faustus's speech to Helen and his final soliloquy. His address to Helen begins with the famous line "Was this the face that launched a thousand ships," referring to the Trojan War, which was fought over Helen, and goes on to list all the great things that Faustus would do to win her love (12.81). He compares himself to the heroes of Greek mythology, who went to war for her hand, and he ends with a lengthy praise of her beauty. In its flowery language and emotional power, the speech marks a return to the eloquence that marks Faustus's words in earlier scenes, before his language and behavior become mediocre and petty. Having squandered his powers in pranks and childish entertainments, Faustus regains his eloquence and tragic grandeur in the final scene, as his doom approaches. Still, asimpressive as this speech is, Faustus maintains the same blind spots that lead him down his dark road in the first place. Earlier, he seeks transcendence through magic instead of religion. Now, he seeks it through sex and female beauty, as he asks Helen to make him "immortal" by kissing him (12.83). Moreover, it is not even clear that Helen is real, since Faustus's earlier conjuring of historical figures evokes only illusions and not physical beings. If Helen too is just an illusion, then Faustus is wasting his last hours dallying with a fantasy image, an apt symbol for his entire life.

Faustus's final speech is the most emotionally powerful scene in the play, as his despairing mind rushes from idea to idea. One moment he is begging time to slow down, the next he is imploring Christ for mercy. One moment he is crying out in fear and trying to hide from the wrath of God, the next he is begging to have the eternity of hell lessened somehow. He curses his parents for giving birth to him but then owns up to his responsibility and curses himself. His mind's various attempts to escape his doom, then, lead inexorably to an understanding of his own guilt.

The passion of the final speech points to the central question in *Doctor Faustus* of why Faustus does not repent. Early in the play, he deceives himself into believing either that hell is not so bad or that it does not exist. But, by the close, with the gates of hell literally opening before him, he still ignores the warnings of his own conscience and of the old man, a physical embodiment of the conscience that plagues him. Faustus's loyalty to Lucifer could be explained by the fact that he is afraid of having his body torn apart by Mephastophilis. But he seems almost eager, even in the next-to-last scene, to reseal his vows in blood, and he even goes a step further when he demands that Mephastophilis punish the old man who urges him to repent. Marlowe suggests that Faustus's self-delusion persists even at the end. Having served Lucifer for so long, he has reached a point at which he cannot imagine breaking free.

In his final speech, Faustus is clearly wracked with remorse, yet he no longer seems to be able to repent. Christian doctrine holds that one can repent for any sin, however grave, up until the moment of death and be saved. Yet this principle does not seem to hold for Marlowe's protagonist. *Doctor Faustus* is a Christian tragedy, but the logic of the final scene is not Christian. Some critics have tried to deal with this problem by claiming that Faustus does not actually repent in the final speech but that he only speaks wistfully about the possibility of repentance. Such an argument, however, is difficult to reconcile with lines such as:

> O, I'll leap up to my God! Who pulls me down?
> . . .
> One drop of blood would save my soul, half a drop: ah my
> Christ—
> (13.69–71)

Faustus appears to be calling on Christ, seeking the precious drop of blood that will save his soul. Yet some unseen force—whether inside or outside him—prevents him from giving himself to God.

Ultimately, the ending of *Doctor Faustus* represents a clash between Christianity, which holds that repentance and salvation are always possible, and the dictates of tragedy, in which some character flaw cannot be corrected, even by appealing to God. The idea of Christian tragedy, then, is paradoxical, as Christianity is ultimately uplifting. People may suffer—as Christ himself did—but for those who repent, salvation eventually awaits. To make *Doctor Faustus* a true tragedy, then, Marlowe had to set down a moment beyond which Faustus could no longer repent, so that in the final scene, while still alive, he can be damned and conscious of his damnation.

The unhappy Faustus's last line returns us to the clash between Renaissance values and medieval values that dominates the early scenes and then recedes as Faustus pursues his mediocre amusements in later scenes. His cry, as he pleads for salvation, that he will burn his books suggests, for the first time since early scenes, that his pact with Lucifer is primarily about a thirst for limitless knowledge—a thirst that is presented as incompatible with Christianity. Scholarship can be Christian, the play suggests, but only within limits. As the Chorus says in its final speech:

> Faustus is gone! Regard his hellish fall,
> Whose fiendful fortune may exhort the wise
> Only to wonder at unlawful things:
> Whose deepness doth entice such forward wits
> To practice more than heavenly power permits.
> (Epilogue.4–8)

In the duel between Christendom and the rising modern spirit, Marlowe's play seems to come down squarely on the side of Christianity. Yet Marlowe, himself notoriously accused of atheism and various other sins, may have had other ideas, and he made his Faustus sympathetic, if not necessarily admirable. While his play shows how the untrammeled pursuit of knowledge and power can be corrupting, it also shows the grandeur of such a quest. Faustus is damned, but the gates that he opens remain standing wide, waiting for others to follow.

SUMMARY & ANALYSIS

Important Quotations Explained

1. The reward of sin is death? That's hard.
    Si peccasse negamus, fallimur, et nulla est in nobis veritas.
    If we say that we have no sin,
    We deceive ourselves, and there's no truth in us.
    Why then belike we must sin,
    And so consequently die.
    Ay, we must die an everlasting death.
    What doctrine call you this? Che sarà, sarà:
    What will be, shall be! Divinity, adieu!
    These metaphysics of magicians,
    And necromantic books are heavenly!
    (1.40–50)

Faustus speaks these lines near the end of his opening soliloquy. In this speech, he considers various fields of study one by one, beginning with logic and proceeding through medicine and law. Seeking the highest form of knowledge, he arrives at theology and opens the Bible to the New Testament, where he quotes from Romans and the first book of John. He reads that "[t]he reward of sin is death," and that "[i]f we say we that we have no sin, / We deceive ourselves, and there's no truth in us." The logic of these quotations—everyone sins, and sin leads to death—makes it seem as though Christianity can promise only death, which leads Faustus to give in to the fatalistic "What will be, shall be! Divinity, adieu!" However, Faustus neglects to read the very next line in John, which states, "If we confess our sins, [God] is faithful and just to forgive us our sins, and to cleanse us from all unrighteousness" (1 John 1:9). By ignoring this passage, Faustus ignores the possibility of redemption, just as he ignores it throughout the play. Faustus has blind spots; he sees what he wants to see rather than what is really there. This blindness is apparent in the very next line of his speech: having turned his back on heaven, he pretends that "[t]hese metaphysics of magicians, / And necromantic books are heavenly." He thus inverts the cosmos, making black magic "heavenly" and religion the source of "everlasting death."

2.   MEPHASTOPHILIS: Why this is hell, nor am I out of it.
     Think'st thou that I, who saw the face of God,
     And tasted the eternal joys of heaven,
     Am not tormented with ten thousand hells
     In being deprived of everlasting bliss?
     O Faustus, leave these frivolous demands,
     Which strike a terror to my fainting soul.

     FAUSTUS: What, is great Mephastophilis so passionate
     For being deprivèd of the joys of heaven?
     Learn thou of Faustus manly fortitude,
     And scorn those joys thou never shalt possess.
        (3.76–86)

This exchange shows Faustus at his most willfully blind, as he listens to Mephastophilis describe how awful hell is for him even as a devil, and as he then proceeds to dismiss Mephastophilis's words blithely, urging him to have "manly fortitude." But the dialogue also shows Mephastophilis in a peculiar light. We know that he is committed to Faustus's damnation—he has appeared to Faustus because of his hope that Faustus will renounce God and swear allegiance to Lucifer. Yet here Mephastophilis seems to be urging Faustus against selling his soul, telling him to "leave these frivolous demands, / Which strike a terror to my fainting soul." There is a parallel between the experience of Mephastophilis and that of Faustus. Just as Faustus now is, Mephastophilis was once prideful and rebelled against God; like Faustus, he is damned forever for his sin. Perhaps because of this connection, Mephastophilis cannot accept Faustus's cheerful dismissal of hell in the name of "manly fortitude." He knows all too well the terrible reality, and this knowledge drives him, in spite of himself, to warn Faustus away from his terrible course.

3. MEPHASTOPHILIS.: Hell hath no limits, nor is
    circumscribed
    In one self-place; for where we are is hell,
    And where hell is, there must we ever be.
    . . .
    All places shall be hell that is not heaven.

    FAUSTUS: Come, I think hell's a fable.

    MEPHASTOPHILIS.: Ay, think so still, till experience
    change thy mind.
    . . .

    FAUSTUS: Think'st thou that Faustus is so fond to imagine
    That after this life there is any pain?
    Tush, these are trifles and mere old wives' tales.
    (5.120–135)

This exchange again shows Mephastophilis warning Faustus about
the horrors of hell. This time, though, their exchange is less significant for what Mephastophilis says about hell than for Faustus's
response to him. Why anyone would make a pact with the devil is
one of the most vexing questions surrounding *Doctor Faustus*, and
here we see part of Marlowe's explanation. We are constantly given
indications that Faustus doesn't really understand what he is doing.
He is a secular Renaissance man, so disdainful of traditional religion
that he believes hell to be a "fable" even when he is conversing with
a devil. Of course, such a belief is difficult to maintain when one is
trafficking in the supernatural, but Faustus has a fallback position.
Faustus takes Mephastophilis's assertion that hell will be "[a]ll
places … that is not heaven" to mean that hell will just be a continuation of life on earth. He fails to understand the difference between
him and Mephastophilis: unlike Mephastophilis, who has lost
heaven permanently, Faustus, despite his pact with Lucifer, is not yet
damned and still has the possibility of repentance. He cannot yet
understand the torture against which Mephastophilis warns him,
and imagines, fatally, that he already knows the worst of what hell
will be.

4.   Was this the face that launched a thousand ships,
      And burnt the topless towers of Ilium?
      Sweet Helen, make me immortal with a kiss:
      Her lips sucks forth my soul, see where it flies!
      Come Helen, come, give me my soul again.
      Here will I dwell, for heaven be in these lips,
      And all is dross that is not Helena!
      (12.81–87)

These lines come from a speech that Faustus makes as he nears the
end of his life and begins to realize the terrible nature of the bargain
he has made. Despite his sense of foreboding, Faustus enjoys his
powers, as the delight he takes in conjuring up Helen makes clear.
While the speech marks a return to the eloquence that he shows
early in the play, Faustus continues to display the same blind spots
and wishful thinking that characterize his behavior throughout the
drama. At the beginning of the play, he dismisses religious transcendence in favor of magic; now, after squandering his powers in petty,
self-indulgent behavior, he looks for transcendence in a woman, one
who may be an illusion and not even real flesh and blood. He seeks
heavenly grace in Helen's lips, which can, at best, offer only earthly
pleasure. "[M]ake me immortal with a kiss," he cries, even as he
continues to keep his back turned to his only hope for escaping damnation—namely, repentance.

QUOTATIONS

5.   Ah Faustus,
     Now hast thou but one bare hour to live,
     And then thou must be damned perpetually.
        . . .
     The stars move still, time runs, the clock w.
     The devil will come, and Faustus must be damned.
     O I'll leap up to my God! Who pulls me down?
     See, see where Christ's blood streams in the firmament!
     One drop would save my soul, half a drop: ah my Christ—
     Ah, rend not my heart for naming of my Christ;
     Yet will I call on him—O spare me, Lucifer!
        . . .
     Earth, gape! O no, it will not harbor me.
     You stars that reigned at my nativity,
     Whose influence hath allotted death and hell,
     Now draw up Faustus like a foggy mist
     Into the entrails of yon laboring cloud,
     That when you vomit forth into the air
     My limbs may issue from your smoky mouths,
     So that my soul may but ascend to heaven.
        . . .
     O God, if thou wilt not have mercy on my soul,
        . . .
     Let Faustus live in hell a thousand years,
     A hundred thousand, and at last be saved.
        . . .
     Cursed be the parents that engendered me:
     No, Faustus, curse thy self, curse Lucifer,
     That hath deprived thee of the joys of heaven.
        . . .
     My God, my God, look not so fierce on me!
        . . .
     Ugly hell gape not! Come not, Lucifer!
     I'll burn my books—ah, Mephastophilis!
        (13.57–113)

QUOTATIONS

These lines come from Faustus's final speech, just before the devils take him down to hell. It is easily the most dramatic moment in the play, and Marlowe uses some of his finest rhetoric to create an unforgettable portrait of the mind of a man about to carried off to a horrific doom. Faustus goes from one idea to another, desperately

.king a way out. But no escape is available, and he ends by reach-
.ng an understanding of his own guilt: "No, Faustus, curse thy self,
curse Lucifer, / That hath deprived thee of the joys of heaven." This
final speech raises the question of why Faustus does not repent earlier and, more importantly, why his desperate cries to Christ for
mercy are not heard. In a truly Christian framework, Faustus would
be allowed a chance at redemption even at the very end. But Marlowe's play ultimately proves more tragic than Christian, and so
there comes a point beyond which Faustus can no longer be saved.
He is damned, in other words, while he is still alive.

Faustus's last line aptly expresses the play's representation of a
clash between Renaissance and medieval values. "I'll burn my
books," Faustus cries as the devils come for him, suggesting, for the
first time since scene 2, when his slide into mediocrity begins, that
his pact with Lucifer is about gaining limitless knowledge, an ambition that the Renaissance spirit celebrated but that medieval Christianity denounced as an expression of sinful human pride. As he is
carried off to hell, Faustus seems to give in to the Christian worldview, denouncing, in a desperate attempt to save himself, the quest
for knowledge that has defined most of his life.

KEY FACTS

FULL TITLE
Published initially as *The Tragicall History of D. Faustus*,
then as *The Tragicall History of the Life and Death of
Doctor Faustus*

AUTHOR
Christopher Marlowe

TYPE OF WORK
Play

GENRE
Tragedy

LANGUAGE
English

TIME AND PLACE WRITTEN
Early 1590s; England

DATE OF FIRST PUBLICATION
The A text was first published in 1604, the B text in 1616.

PUBLISHER
Uncertain; possibly Philip Henslowe, a theatrical entrepreneur

NARRATOR
None for the most part, but the Chorus, which appears
intermittently between scenes, provides background
information and comments on the action

POINT OF VIEW
While he sometimes cedes the stage to the Chorus or the lesser,
comic characters, Faustus is central figure in the play, and he
has several long soliloquies that let us see things from his point of
view.

TONE
Grandiose and tragic, with occasional moments of low comedy

TENSE
The Chorus, who provides the only narration, alternates between the present and past tenses.

SETTING (TIME)
The 1580s

SETTING (PLACE)
Europe, specifically Germany and Italy

PROTAGONIST
Doctor Faustus

MAJOR CONFLICT
Faustus sells his soul to Lucifer in exchange for twenty-four years of immense power, but the desire to repent begins to plague him as the fear of hell grows in him.

RISING ACTION
Faustus's study of dark magic and his initial conversations with Mephastophilis

CLIMAX
Faustus's sealing of the pact that promises his soul to Lucifer

FALLING ACTION
Faustus's traveling of the world and performing of magic for various rulers

THEMES
Sin, redemption, and damnation; the conflict between medieval and Renaissance values; absolute power and corruption; the dividedness of human nature

MOTIFS
Magic and the supernatural; practical jokes

SYMBOLS
Blood; Faustus's rejection of the ancient authorities; the good angel and the evil angel

FORESHADOWING
The play constantly hints at Faustus's ultimate damnation. His blood congeals when he tries to sign away his soul; the words Homo fuge, meaning "Fly, man!", appear on his arm after he makes the pact; and he is constantly tormented by misgivings and fears of hell.

KEY FACTS

STUDY QUESTIONS & ESSAY TOPICS

STUDY QUESTIONS

1. *Is Doctor Faustus a Christian tragedy? Why or why not?*

Doctor Faustus has elements of both Christian morality and classical tragedy. On the one hand, it takes place in an explicitly Christian cosmos: God sits on high, as the judge of the world, and every soul goes either to hell or to heaven. There are devils and angels, with the devils tempting people into sin and the angels urging them to remain true to God. Faustus's story is a tragedy in Christian terms, because he gives in to temptation and is damned to hell. Faustus's principal sin is his great pride and ambition, which can be contrasted with the Christian virtue of humility; by letting these traits rule his life, Faustus allows his soul to be claimed by Lucifer, Christian cosmology's prince of devils.

Yet while the play seems to offer a very basic Christian message—that one should avoid temptation and sin, and repent if one cannot avoid temptation and sin—its conclusion can be interpreted as straying from orthodox Christianity in order to conform to the structure of tragedy. In a traditional tragic play, as pioneered by the Greeks and imitated by William Shakespeare, a hero is brought low by an error or series of errors and realizes his or her mistake only when it is too late. In Christianity, though, as long as a person is alive, there is always the possibility of repentance—so if a tragic hero realizes his or her mistake, he or she may still be saved even at the last moment. But though Faustus, in the final, wrenching scene, comes to his senses and begs for a chance to repent, it is too late, and he is carried off to hell. Marlowe rejects the Christian idea that it is never too late to repent in order to increase the dramatic power of his finale, in which Faustus is conscious of his damnation and yet, tragically, can do nothing about it.

2. *Scholar R.M. Dawkins once called Faustus "a
    Renaissance man who had to pay the medieval price for
    being one." Do you think this is an accurate
    characterization of Marlowe's tragic hero?*

Doctor Faustus has frequently been interpreted as depicting a clash
between the values of the medieval world and the emerging spirit of
the sixteenth-century Renaissance. In medieval Europe, Christianity and God lay at the center of intellectual life: scientific inquiry lan-
guished, and theology was known as "the queen of the sciences." In
art and literature, the emphasis was on the lives of the saints and the
mighty rather than on those of ordinary people. With the advent of
the Renaissance, however, there was a new celebration of the free
individual and the scientific exploration of nature.

While Marlowe's Faustus is, admittedly, a magician and not a scientist, this distinction was not so clearly drawn in the sixteenth century as it is today. (Indeed, famous scientists such as Isaac Newton
dabbled in astrology and alchemy into the eighteenth century.) With
his rejection of God's authority and his thirst for knowledge and
control over nature, Faustus embodies the more secular spirit of the
dawning modern era. Marlowe symbolizes this spirit in the play's
first scene, when Faustus explicitly rejects all the medieval authorities—Aristotle in logic, Galen in medicine, Justinian in law, and the
Bible in religion—and decides to strike out on his own. In this
speech, Faustus puts the medieval world to bed and steps firmly into
the new era. Yet, as the quote says, he "pay[s] the medieval price"
for taking this new direction, since he still exists firmly within a
Christian framework, meaning that his transgressions ultimately
condemn him to hell.

In the play's final lines, the Chorus tells us to view Faustus's fate
as a warning and not follow his example. This admonition would
seem to make Marlowe a defender of the established religious values, showing us the terrible fate that awaits a Renaissance man who
rejects God. But by investing Faustus with such tragic grandeur,
Marlowe may be suggesting a different lesson. Perhaps the price of
rejecting God is worth it, or perhaps Faustus pays the price for all of
western culture, allowing it to enter a new, more secular era.

3. *Discuss the character of Mephastophilis. How much
of a role does he play in Faustus's damnation? How
does Marlowe complicate his character and inspire
our sympathy?*

Mephastophilis is part of a long tradition of fascinating literary devils that reached its peak a century later with John Milton's portrayal
of Satan in *Paradise Lost,* published in the late seventeenth century.
Mephastophilis seems to desire Faustus's damnation: he appears
eagerly when Faustus rejects God and firms up Faustus's resolve
when Faustus hedges on his contract with Lucifer. Yet there is an
odd ambivalence in Mephastophilis. Before the pact is sealed, he
actually warns Faustus against making the deal, telling him how
awful the pains of hell are. In a famous passage, when Faustus
remarks that Mephastophilis seems to be free of hell at the moment,
Mephastophilis retorts,

> Why this is hell, nor am I out of it.
> Think'st thou that I, who saw the face of God,
> And tasted the eternal joys of heaven,
> Am not tormented with ten thousand hells
> In being deprived of everlasting bliss?
> (3.76–80)

Again, when Faustus expresses skepticism that any afterlife exists,
Mephastophilis assures him that hell is real and terrible. These odd
complications in Mephastophilis's character serve a twofold pur-
pose. First, they highlight Faustus's willful blindness, since he dismisses the warning of the very demon with whom he is bartering
over his soul. In this regard, his remark that hell is a myth seems particularly delusional. At the same time, these complications inspire a
kind of pity for Mephastophilis and his fellow devils, who are
damned to hell just as surely as Faustus or any other sinful, unrepen-
tant human. These devils may be villains, but they are tragic figures,
separated forever from the bliss of God's presence by their pride.
Indeed, Mephastophilis and Faust are similar figures: both reject
God out of pride, and both suffer for it eternally.

SUGGESTED ESSAY TOPICS

1. How does Faustus use the magical gifts that he receives? How are the uses to which he puts his powers significant? What do they suggest about his character or about the nature of unlimited power?

2. What is the role of the comic characters—Robin, Rafe, the horse-courser, and the clown, for example? How does Marlowe use them to illuminate Faustus's decline?

3. When does Faustus have misgivings about his pact with Lucifer? What makes him desire to repent? Why do you think he fails to repent?

4. Is God present in the play? If so, where? If not, what does God's absence suggest?

5. Discuss the role of Faustus's soliloquies—particularly his speeches about the different kinds of knowledge in scene 1 and his long soliloquies in scene 12—in shaping our understanding of his character.

6. Is Faustus misled by the devils, or is he willfully blind to the reality of his situation?

REVIEW & RESOURCES

QUIZ

1. In the Prologue, who introduces the story of *Doctor Faustus*?

   A. The Chorus
   B. Faustus
   C. Mephastophilis
   D. Wagner

2. To which Greek mythological character is Faustus compared in the Prologue?

   A. Hercules
   B. Perseus
   C. Icarus
   D. Theseus

3. What fields of learning does Faustus consider before he turns to magic?

   A. Chemistry, biology, and physics
   B. Logic, medicine, law, and theology
   C. Navigation, astronomy, rhetoric, and theology
   D. Grammar, history, science, and Latin

4. Which characters instruct Faustus in the dark arts?

   A. The scholars
   B. Wagner and Robin
   C. The good and bad angels
   D. Cornelius and Valdes

5. When he first summons Mephastophilis, how does Faustus ask him to appear?

   A. In the shape of a Franciscan friar
   B. In the shape of a beautiful woman
   C. As a winged creature with horns
   D. As a handsome young man

6. What is the name of the ruler of hell in *Doctor Faustus*?

    A. Satan
    B. Mephastophilis
    C. Lucifer
    D. Belzebub

7. How long does Faustus demand that Mephastophilis serve him?

    A. Thirty years
    B. Twenty-four years
    C. One hour
    D. A century

8. What does Faustus offer in return for this service?

    A. All his riches
    B. The life of his first-born child
    C. Nothing
    D. His soul

9. How does Faustus sign his compact with Lucifer?

    A. In his own blood
    B. In the blood of a virgin
    C. In ink produced in hell
    D. He doesn't

10. What is the meaning of the words that appear on Faustus's arm in Latin?

    A. "Satan's own"
    B. "Prince of Darkness"
    C. "Fly, man"
    D. "You are doomed"

11. Who agrees, under duress, to become Wagner's servant?

    A. Faustus
    B. The clown
    C. Belzebub
    D. Helen of Troy

12. What does Mephastophilis refuse to tell Faustus?

    A.   If Faustus will be damned

    B.   How many planets there are

    C.   Where hell is located

    D.   Who made the world

13. Why does Mephastophilis refuse to answer this question?

    A.   He says that the answer is "against our kingdom"

    B.   He does not know the answer

    C.   He thinks that the answer is too terrifying forFaustus to hear

    D.   He thinks that God will strike him down if heanswers the question

14. Which city does Faustus visit extensively in scene 7?

    A.   Amsterdam

    B.   Berlin

    C.   Rome

    D.   Jerusalem

15. What trick does Faustus, while invisible, play on the pope?

    A.   He makes a Bible burn in the pope's hands

    B.   He exposes the pope's baldness

    C.   He fools the pope into believing a statue istalking to him

    D.   He steals dishes of food and disrupts thepope's banquet

16. Which historical figure does Faustus conjure up for the emperor to see?

    A.   Helen of Troy

    B.   Jesus Christ

    C.   Joan of Arc

    D.   Alexander the Great

17. Which character is publicly skeptical of Faustus's powers?

    A.   Charles V
    B.   The knight (also known as Benvolio)
    C.   The horse-courser
    D.   The ostler

18. How does Faustus humiliate this skeptic?

    A.   He turns his skin green
    B.   He makes him unable to speak
    C.   He makes antlers sprout from the skeptic's head
    D.   He hypnotizes him and makes him strip naked

19. Who tries to persuade Faustus to repent just before he reseals his pact with Lucifer?

    A.   An old man
    B.   Wagner
    C.   Mephastophilis
    D.   The knight

20. What happens to the horse that Faustus sells to the horse-courser?

    A.   It turns into a dragon
    B.   It dies immediately
    C.   It lives a long and healthy life
    D.   It turns into a heap of straw when it goes in the water

21. What does the horse-courser think he is removing from Faustus's body after Faustus wakes?

    A.   His shirt
    B.   His leg
    C.   His cloak
    D.   His hand

22. What does Faustus fetch for the Duchess of Vanholt?

    A.   A male slave
    B.   A griffin
    C.   A dish of grapes
    D.   A horse

23. Where, according to Mephastophilis, is hell?

    A. Everywhere that heaven is not
    B. Deep below the earth's surface
    C. Inside Faustus's soul
    D. Directly beneath heaven

24. What famous beauty does Mephastophilis present to Faustus in scene 12?

    A. Joan of Arc
    B. Eleanor of Aquitaine
    C. Catherine the Great
    D. Helen of Troy

25. What happens to Faustus at the end of the play?

    A. He repents and is saved
    B. He kills himself
    C. He becomes emperor of Germany
    D. He is carried off to hell

SUGGESTIONS FOR FURTHER READING

BLOOM, HAROLD. *Christopher Marlowe*. New York: Chelsea House, 1986.

FARNHAM, WILLARD. *Twentieth-Century Interpretations of* DOCTOR FAUSTUS. Englewood Cliffs, New Jersey: Prentice-Hall, 1969.

GREENBLATT, STEPHEN. *Renaissance Self-Fashioning: From More to Shakespeare*. Chicago: University of Chicago Press, 1980.

MACLURE, MILLAR, ED. *Marlowe: The Critical Heritage*. Boston: Routledge, 1979.

MARLOWE, CHRISTOPHER. DOCTOR FAUSTUS. Ed. Sylvan Barnet. New York: Signet, 2001.

SALES, ROGER. *Christopher Marlowe*. New York: St. Martin's Press, 1991.

TYDEMAN, WILLIAM. DOCTOR FAUSTUS: *Text and Performance*. Basingstoke, England: Macmillan, 1984.